P. Batzell

JOOP VAN DAM was a Medical Doctor for 40 years in Haarlem, the Netherlands. Now retired, he is still active as a lecturer in educational and medical programmes, and in the Anthroposophical Society in the Netherlands, of which he was President for seven years. He is the author of several publications, including *The Sixfold Path*.

THE EIGHTFOLD PATH

A Way of Development for those Working in Education, Therapy and the Caring Professions

Joop van Dam

TEMPLE LODGE

Temple Lodge Publishing Ltd.
Hillside House, The Square
Forest Row, RH18 5ES

www.templelodge.com

First published in English by Temple Lodge Publishing, 2016

Originally published in Dutch under the title *Het achtvoudige pad* by Antroposofische Zorg, Netherlands, 2013

Translated by Dirkje and Otto Koene

© Joop van Dam 2013
This translation © Temple Lodge Publishing 2016

This book is copyright under the Berne Convention. All rights reserved. Apart from any fair dealing for the purpose of private study, research, criticism or review, no part of this publication may be reproduced, stored in a retrieval system, or transmitted in any form or by any means, electronic, electrical, chemical, mechanical, optical, photocopying, recording or otherwise, without the prior written permission of the copyright owner. Inquiries should be addressed to the Publishers

The right of Joop van Dam to be identified as the author of this work has been asserted in accordance with sections 77 and 78 of the Copyright, Designs and Patents Act, 1988

A CIP catalogue record for this book is available from the British Library

ISBN 978 1 906999 88 9

Cover by Morgan Creative
Typeset by DP Photosetting, Neath, West Glamorgan
Printed and bound by 4Edge Ltd., Essex

Contents

Introduction   1

1. The Right View   5
2. The Right Resolve   9
3. The Right Word   11
4. The Right Action   13
5. The Right Standpoint   15
6. The Right Effort   17
7. The Right Remembrance   19
8. The Right Contemplation   21

Practising the Eightfold Path   23
The Profession of the Therapist   27
How Does the Eightfold Path Work?   39
The Relation to the Days of the Week   41
The Sixth Century BC: The 'Hinge' of Time   45

Introduction

What role can the Eightfold Path play with regard to the profession of the therapist?

It is known that the writer of the Gospel of Luke was a physician. At a later date Luke also became the patron saint of healers as well as painters. This is not surprising. There is no Gospel which contains the description of so many healings, and where this is done in such a careful and detailed manner. And these healings, as well as other events, particularly from Jesus' youth, inspired painters throughout the ages to create works of art, helping those who viewed them to have new and intimate experiences — experiences which put the soul into motion and provided it with nutriment and healing. The Gospel of Luke evokes the forces of compassion and love.

Six centuries prior to the events described in the New Testament, the Buddha had already introduced to the world the teaching of love and compassion. This teaching originated from the confrontation which the Buddha had with the suffering in the world. After a protected youth within the confines of the park-style dwellings of his father, he took the initiative to go out into the world and there he came to know suffering, illness and death. While digesting these forceful experiences, the Buddha gained the insight into the cause of suffering and he looked for a way to eliminate this.

The cause lay within the soul, which, in the course of time, had been exposed to all sorts of temptations and had become ever more self-centred and egotistic. Man had become unfree in his association with his environment. For the purification and transformation of the soul (the astral body in anthroposophical terminology), the Buddha inaugurated the Eightfold Path. Eight exercises were given, which could lead to a new relationship with the world. Instead of being self-centred, a warm interest developed in one's environment. This new attitude helped to develop the forces of love and compassion.

What the Buddha had offered as a teaching became daily practice in the way Christ worked; it was done. Doctrine became life.

This small book describes experiences which can be gained as one sets foot onto the Eightfold Path. Also, what happens when one practises these exercises in their therapeutic work is explored. A starting point for these exercises is the description in the book by Rudolf Steiner *Knowledge of the Higher Worlds and its Attainment*, and his third lecture in the series about the Gospel of Luke.

The exercises have a specific sequence. Each exercise is, as it were, a precondition for the next. Each enables the next step, forming its foundation.

1. The Right View

The first exercise concerns thinking. Already in the time of the Buddha, schooling started with the most conscious part of man: the awake, clear-thinking consciousness. This is also the case with the exercises of the twelve-petalled lotus flower (the Sixfold Path). The exercises begin with the ability to control one's thinking. The Sixfold Path focuses, in the first instance, on the thinking process, which is being strengthened by means of thinking about common utensils in everyday life. For the Eightfold Path, it is the result of thinking that is important: the view that is formed. One seeks to arrive at the right view. The purification of the astral body starts here. For a long time, reacting to something being perceived (by way of a judgement, a word, or an action) is held back. Ever new and pure observations enable a rich and growing picture to be formed. Each freshly acquired detail brings the moment closer, where the total of the observations begins to 'speak'. The degree of receptivity of the soul to impressions coming from the outside world is determined also by past experiences and, in particular, the extent to which one has come to terms with these. Some experiences with colours or tones or compositions can have made the soul so lively and versatile that this has become conducive to making subsequent observations in the same field. They have strengthened in the soul the capacity to observe. However, the reverse can also happen. An experience in relation to the world can be so overwhelming, can call for such dismay, that the soul is wounded and turns away. Coming to terms with what has happened does not take place in such a case and results in oversensitivity. A disorder in the perception organ has now occurred.

From the Buddhist point of view, such a shocking experience could not have its roots just in this life, but also in previous lives. As to your ability to perceive, this sets you off on the wrong foot. And instead of being unprejudiced you no longer have the ability to look at things with an open mind. In our encounter with the world, sympathies and antipathies, of which we are only partly aware, are poor companions. An important goal of the Eightfold Path was to free the soul, in its relationship with the world, from disturbing influences of previous incarnations.

To get a clear view of something, this something must be given a chance to show itself in as many ways as possible. Consent or disapproval need to be avoided. Instead, you seek to look at something from several vantage points. The Wadden Sea[*] has, for instance, aesthetical, biological, economic and numerous other aspects. You seek to distinguish between the essential and the unessential, to make sure that the view represents the real issues at stake. The inner activity which is unfolded thereby leads to views that are meaningful. This is to be taken seriously because your view starts to carry weight. That is why this first step is also called the right opinion. That is, the view which is not just a recorded observation, but one which is the result of your inner activity. This is an activity which has resulted in a picture which is as complete as possible, one which you fully support and does justice in your opinion to the matter involved.

Views can change in the course of time; they can also differ from place to place. A family of today is different from a family a century ago. A family in an Italian village differs from a family in an American city. Consequently, it is sensible to reassess views regularly to make sure they are up-to-date.

---

[*] The shallow, tidal waters in between the string of islands and the Dutch coast in the north-west of the Netherlands.

2. The Right Resolve

The next step is the right judgement, which is also known as the right resolve. The relationship between resolve and judgement is similar to the relationship between view and opinion. What resolve and opinion have in common is that they both place particular emphasis on the direction of the will; they both have an existential character. A resolve and a decision both precede taking action; they still work internally and are preparatory steps for taking action. What is paramount is that thoughtless action is prevented from being taken. During this decision-making process one seeks to arrive at a balanced inner judgement about a given situation, whereby one can make a decision. All our actions ought to be reasonable, they must have a reason; without having a well-considered motive, an action must be abstained from being taken. When a judgement leads on to a decision we can also stick to it, when we proceed with the execution. After the right view, a view which has to be as complete as possible, a value category is added to the right judgement: is it true or not true, beautiful or ugly, good or bad? Such a judgement is the result of a process that involves the entire soul and that leads to a resolution. The judging consciousness connects itself with 'heart and soul' with the relevant fact or circumstance. This is comparable to the step from idea to ideal. In an inner sense there is no longer any space between the 'I' and the world.

Personal considerations are sacrificed for the right judgement. The way to the world is thereby opened. Once again we free ourselves from what connects us to the past, by way of personal preferences or dislikes. Also, this second exercise is a purification of the astral body. This is the beginning of an initiative, one which is still entirely internal.

3. The Right Word

Now comes the third step: the right word. It builds on what has first been formed as the right view and which subsequently has formed the right resolve. Now something of us comes out in the open. We express ourselves. This can be with a word; it can also be a sign, a gesture. There are many ways to express this. And once again, every expression is well considered; it is as it were laid on a scale in order to find the right balance. For instance, is it meaningful to say something or is it more fruitful to remain silent? Only what is significant is to be said. Speaking for the sake of speaking must be abstained from. The use of jargon also belongs in this category of 'idle talk'. Using jargon often indicates that you are not yet able (or willing) to express a thought in words. In Buddhism, where abstention from speaking is concerned, the specific instruction was also given for one not to lie, not to scold or hurt and not to speak evil. These are specific, practical exercises.

In a good conversation often the pauses form a precondition for a fruitful continuation. Sometimes listening in silence can be encouraging for another person. In German one calls this a *beredtes Schweigen* ('purposeful silence'). To which remarks of another should you respond and which allegations (or even questions) should you ignore? In a group conversation when do you make a contribution? How can you make sure that you do not talk before it is your turn?

An experienced speaker knows to apply the right measure in his flow of words. He knows from experience that you can use too few words and also too many. The right word stands in between the two.

In social life, communication is one of the fundamental life processes. The astral body can also be called the communication body. It is therefore not surprising that in the purification of the astral body your practising speaking the right word is relevant. Communicating, however, is both speaking and listening. Part of this third step of the Eightfold Path is asking questions. Thereby the other can speak the right word.

4. The Right Action

The right word is followed by the right action. It concerns the actions which take place in the outside world. Again there is the search to find a balance between that which you wish to do out of an inner impulse and acting in response to something from the outside. You are striving to find the middle between both. When we are young (the sentient soul) we have the ability to react spontaneously to what is happening in the world. Later on in life (the consciousness soul) our actions are directed much more out of conscientious necessity which has developed internally. The right action is born out of reconciling the external and internal worlds. Bringing both into harmony is being strived for. Then you can be present 'in' your action with full conviction.

Where an inner initiative is concerned, you consider what the impact on others will be. Is it actually feeding the ego or does it benefit the whole? When a proposed action calls forth resistance, this can be a reason to abstain from performing it. However, giving something further thought and reconsideration can also lead to the decision to proceed further — particularly when you are convinced that after an unpleasant beginning the action will ultimately result in a positive development.

Conversely, where it concerns an action which is brought forth from the outside world, it is good to assess whether it is in keeping with one's own possibilities and intentions. When this is the case, you can honestly, and with conviction, proceed forth and feel inwardly connected with it. However, when this is not the case, you must also be able to abstain from cooperating with the initiative taken by another. Also the conscious decision not to act is an action.

When acting, the right balance lies also in applying the right amount of effort. You can just do a minimum, pay lip service to something, or you can also do too much. Being addicted to working in the world, being a workaholic, means that you are not sufficiently aware of your own being.

You can also look at an action from a time perspective. Priority: which action should be given priority? Topicality: is this the right moment to act, or is it better to wait? And finally: is the action complete? A finished job provides energy for new actions.

5. The Right Standpoint

The right action is the next step along the way that leads from the inside (first the view, then the resolve) to the outside, by way of speaking the right word. By taking this fifth step, the action is continued, but at the same time it forms the beginning of a movement towards the inside. A sense of realization occurs. Am I free in what I do? How does what lives inside of me relate to what is coming towards me from out of the world? Striving for the right standpoint means to exercise the skill of the encounter. What is feasible at this spot (here) and at this moment (now)? How can I inwardly agree with the life situation in which I find myself? Can I follow the example of what a woman ripened by faith said, 'The way it comes is how I want it'?

Initially you can experience the following: I adapt to the situation. Now this can develop into: I do what is fitting in these circumstances and try to achieve the optimum. This fifth step on the Eightfold Path ripens the insight that life is the means which enables development, both of yourself and of the world. In this life and work on earth, there is a constant interaction between heaven and earth, between spirit and matter. In Greek mythology it was the god Mercury who acted as a messenger in facilitating the encounter between both worlds.

In order to take the right standpoint and to work from thereon, it is necessary to look after the conditions of life — to obey the laws of life, and that means to live a healthy life. Our life forces are being maintained and stimulated by using them. After a serious illness, recovery is promoted not only by resting but also with some regularity in undertaking minor activities. Once again, the secret of the right way of handling the use of the life forces is finding the right measure: not to do too much, and also not too little; not to act too fast and also not too slowly. What matters is the right flexibility.

6. The Right Effort

As much as the fifth step must be placed in life at each given moment, the sixth step is one where more time is needed. In a way, you proceed from space (standpoint) to time (striving). What matters are the longer-term intentions. You look beyond the day-to-day events. You rise above the current situation and from the overview you acquire, you plan a course of action.

In doing so, you look into two directions. Firstly you look at what you carry with you from the past—that which you are capable of, your talents. Part of the right striving is that you look for the activities that are fitting for you. Your point of departure is your own possibilities. You are not chasing something which is beyond your possibilities; on the other hand, you also do not settle for what is below your own potential. The right effort is looking for the healthy, individually determined balance.

As well as looking at the past, there is the future perspective. Out of ideals you can set a goal which can be strived for. It can consist of some research you want to perform, it can take the form of exercising a certain attitude towards life; many other intentions are possible. In all cases, what matters is the consistency of effort. You give yourself a certain task, and in sticking to that you create certain time structures in your life and in your work. This leads to the creation of new habits. That is why this phase in the Eightfold Path is also called the right habit. For instance, an outstanding contribution to the health forces in our organism results from cultivating specific habits — and to change these again after a while.

7. The Right Remembrance

The seventh exercise aims at learning as much as possible from life. On the one hand this means that we must take initiatives and gather a lot of experiences, and, on the other hand, that we assess these experiences according to their value. If you have done something improper or wrong, assessing this makes you aware of it. With this knowledge, you try to do the same thing differently the next time round. In this way, life becomes a learning process. In the Netherlands this method has found expression under the motto 'examine your own work', and its fruitfulness has been proven. You can also learn from the experiences of others: of their failures and detours, and also and especially from the quick and effective ways they have found, which you had not yet discovered.

In both cases, where it concerns one's own experiences and those of other people, what matters is that they are looked at in retrospect. The Buddha also called this exercise the right memory. By means of looking at things in retrospect, experiences are digested and an inner enrichment takes place.

Through this enrichment the soul acquires an expansion of her capacity to perceive. Conversely, undigested experiences can be disruptive in our encounter with the world.

Looking at things in retrospect can extend over different periods. The time frame can be an hour, a day, and also years. An actively exercised memory enables experiences offered by life to be employed with an awake consciousness, thus finding in a healthy way a useful place in the soul. In dealing with the past in this manner, the past helps us prepare for the future. This also forms the prelude to the last, all-encompassing exercise.

8. The Right Contemplation

In the so-called basic exercises (also called 'parallel exercises') five distinct regions are successively cultivated under the direction of the 'I' (thinking, willing, feeling, positivity and being open-minded). The sixth exercise consists of combining the preceding exercises and giving them thereby an extra dimension. In a comparable way, different provinces of the soul are permeated in a new fashion by the first seven steps of the Eightfold Path. The last, the eighth exercise brings the previous exercises together and places them on a different level. Seven exercises can (we will come back to this later) be related to the days of the week. The eighth exercise does not have a place in this weekly rhythm and falls, as it were, outside of time. At every moment of the day you can withdraw from daily worries and concerns and turn your attention within for a short time. This is also called the right meditation.

At such moments of introspection you can look back at your life, consult with yourself, and develop self-knowledge. You can discover qualities that are open to change, test your life principles against (the outer and the inner) reality, and reset your goals for the future on the basis of such moments of reflection and inner peace. They offer opportunities to distinguish the important from the unimportant. This can still be strengthened by concentrating on subjects which, while generally human, rise above day-to-day life. Books such as *The Little Prince* by Antoine de Saint-Exupéry, the *Bhagavadgita*, certain poems and the Bible lend themselves to this.

Practising the Eightfold Path

Experience tells us that working with the so-called 'basic exercises' (the Sixfold Path) is more accessible for most people today than practising the Eightfold Path. The basic exercises are 'more practical' in a way. You know that you have been doing them: for a few minutes you have concentrated your thoughts on a utensil; you have identified something positive or examined your feelings. To engage in this is easy enough. When practising the Eightfold Path something else happens. What matters when doing the first exercise, the right view, is the result—that this constitutes the real view which is as objective as possible. With the first basic exercise the most important thing is that you begin to gain control over the thinking process.

The Eightfold Path calls for a special kind of awareness of one's relationship with the world. Is my perception of the world correct? Am I speaking the right word? Is the standpoint I have taken adequate?

With regard to the six basic exercises, faithful persistence is of major importance. As to these exercises, it is advisable to keep doing them consistently for a month, one at a time. To do them must become a habit. It follows for the basic exercises that they ultimately work through the 'habit body', the etheric body. To develop a new habit, the monthly rhythm is a prerequisite.

In the exercises of the Eightfold Path, the week has a central place. Dealing with something in the soul, the astral body, corresponds to the rhythm of a week. Seven of the exercises are connected with a specific weekday and there is one, the eighth, which stands beyond time. You can utilize this relationship with the days of the week and do all of the exercises within a single week, and for a long time in that manner—week in, week out. You then live within the constellation of the exercises; you choose the right moment, in keeping with the terminology of the Eightfold Path. You have as it were the wind at your back. It is also possible that you stick with one exercise for a longer time. This way you intensify the potency, you incite the exercise, thereby making it more transparent and more forceful. In both cases it is meaningful to work with a diary. A diary is a sort of memory aid which facilitates your arriving where you want to be. At the same time you thereby sign your own attendance list each day.

The diary contains the outcome of the retrospective review. And for the very reason that the exercises depend so strongly on your being consciously awake, particularly for the middle three where the right moment to act is passing very quickly, the retrospective review exercise helps to generate and acquire an even stronger presence of mind. Where did I speak the right word (or remain silent)? Where did I act appropriately? Where did I face up to and deal with a situation? And, in doing so, did I manage to find the right standpoint? Other exercises, the first one and the last two, one can still do daily at the time of doing the retrospective review exercise, and thus become ever more familiar with the essence of the activity. You can put the diary aside at a given moment, when it is time for an interval in order to give other exercises a chance also. When resuming the Eightfold Path, you can proceed on the basis of the experiences you have already gained (as shown in the diary).

The Profession of the Therapist

The Eightfold Path begins with schooling the instrument of empathy (called love and compassion by the Buddha). In the profession of the therapist, empathy can be practised directly. This thereby shows very quickly just how meaningful the sequence of the exercises is.

1. The right view lives, for instance, in the idea you have of the heart. What is its function in the blood circulation? Is it the heart that brings the blood into motion? Or is it the other way around? What is its relationship to the other organs and organ systems? For which processes of the soul does the heart serve as an instrument? Also, in the field of the typologies (organ types, hysteria/neurasthenia) the right opinion is important and can lead the observations made in practice to an ever richer and thereby more accurate view. Another way for us to work on meaningful insights concerns the field where the therapeutical remedies are found. Following the progress of a plant through its annual cycle creates the possibility to embed the newly found phenomena in the entirety of the already existing scope of knowledge. A painting therapist can enrich the right view of a particular colour by observing nature or the arts. Likewise the therapeutic eurythmist can tell from experience that the right view towards a certain succession of sounds or a rhythm, or another therapeutic exercise, keeps growing throughout life.

2. The right judgement is something else; it goes a step further. With a judgement you are concerned with something in a way that is different than with a view. That is why it is also called the right resolve. The right view followed by the right judgement has an impact on the action to be taken. Your judgement, with respect to the heart or the constitutional typology of a particular patient you have met, is not non-committal. It has an existential effect on the encounter between you and the other.

For the therapist, it is the step from the perception (view) to the diagnosis. And a true diagnosis is also the decision which leads towards the therapy.

3. The right word offers a golden opportunity for the therapist/physician to practise the Eightfold Path, while having due regard for the professional secrecy that forms part of this. That is the self-evident inner attitude which protects the confidential relationship with the patient, prompting you to remain silent towards others about the experiences you and your patient share together.

Subsequently, what do I and do I not tell the patient? The latter does not have to mean that you keep the patient in a state of dependency. There are considerations about the further progress of the illness which may be of concern to the physician. For the time being, he can keep these concerns to himself so as not to burden the patient with these, as long as there are no concrete indications of there being complicating developments. On the other hand, patients become uncertain when they suspect that specific information, which they can understand, is withheld from them. 'Bad news' in most cases is better given directly. Experience shows that coming to terms with the news given together forms an indispensable part of the communication.

A diagnosis can convey purely technical information, but an illness can also be the expression of a certain lifestyle or signal the beginning of a new phase of life. As a physician, can you speak about the diagnosis in such a way so that the patient, by listening, can discover for himself how he can contribute to his recovery or to a fruitful new development as a result of his lifestyle?

Questions asked of a patient by a therapist can sometimes be of more help than to give directives. The more the right word (a question in this case) contributes to there being a conversation, the more 'emancipated' the patient will be and the greater his own contribution can be in experiencing the illness.

4. Also the right action can consist of not-doing, just as **the right word** can consist of being silent. *Nil nocere* (do no harm): acting in such a way that it does not result in harm. In the *Bhagavadgita*, Arjuna says to the charioteer: 'We must obtain insight into what we do, but we must also be alert about what we are not doing. The essence of the deed is deeply hidden.' The Sanskrit word for deed is karma. Doing something brings about karma, but not doing something brings about karma also. Inoculation against certain diseases is a concrete interference, but abstaining from inoculation can also be considered as a clear form of steering action. Can one place his actions consciously in the stream of karma?

In the realm of this exercise also belongs the choice of the nature of the therapy. As an example, the problem of the suicidal patient can serve. When must a form of restraining freedom be applied (for which the patient may later be grateful) in order to prevent life-threatening situations? When do you place your patient in a state of dependency, thus depriving him or her of the possibility to develop and grow through confrontation with a problem? Compelling therapies are also there in the field of medication. By means of authoritarian medication you do away with the opportunity to mobilize self-healing forces. In most cases of life-threatening situations, a compelling medication will be given priority to keep the possibility of further development open for later. Sometimes there is a possibility of consulting with the patient, but often the physician/therapist is alone in his action. In treading the Eightfold Path, this fourth step is perhaps the most existential.

5. The right standpoint is related to space and time. Doing the right thing depends very much on the situation you are in. You are dealing with the here and now. Having a discussion with a patient in the consulting room is different from a visit to the sickbed. In the latter case it makes a great deal of difference whether you stand or sit at the same level as your patient. The point in time to discuss the therapy is also important. Having a conversation in the morning has a different quality compared with one in the afternoon or evening (what can also be taken into account is whether someone is, constitutionally speaking, a morning or an evening person). Also in medication therapy the moment of application can play a role. Certain medicines you will want to have an 'incarnating' effect, for instance with a mistletoe preparation when treating cancer, with iron or with Gencydo (Citrus/Cydonia comp.). By giving this medication in the morning, you follow the incarnating movement which takes place in the first half of the day anyway. Other medications are more suited for the excarnating phase of the day.

The right 'stand'-point can come to expression in the 'listening'-point. Before you arrive at the right 'stand'-point it is indispensable to listen well. Out of what need does someone speak when they say they do not feel well? Does he have a stomach-ache, a full bladder, or has he just received a letter with bad news? Nurses in particular have a good feel for identifying the area from where the suffering originates.

It is also important to create a situation in which the patient can react positively to the prescribed treatment. For artistic therapies, where the soul actively participates in the healing process, this is a must. In the event of more physically determined measures, a good explanation can help to overcome any inner resistance. Often it will be a matter of what Ita Wegman said about the diet therapy: 'The truth of the diet lies in between the physician and the patient.'

Finding the right standpoint constitutes the supreme art of Mercury, who, with presence of mind, addresses the situation at that very moment and in that specific place. A change in circumstances may necessitate an adjustment to the therapy. And yet there must remain some consistency in the line of treatment.

6. The right effort secures consistency of action in the longer term. It shows the value of having a so-called treatment plan. A treatment plan addresses, on the one hand, the sequence of therapies. After a prolonged use of painkillers or antibiotics, sometimes it can be useful to first reinforce the general creative forces of the organism, for instance by taking Argentum D6 powder three times daily for a period of six weeks prior to commencing a specific medicamental therapy. Also, treatments which the patient undergoes without increased mental effort (like massage or hydrotherapy) can offer him or her the inner possibility and vitality subsequently to engage actively with the soul in an artistic therapy. On the other hand, the treatment plan pays attention to the interplay between the various therapies.

Experience shows that certain medicaments and specific exercises that arise from the artistic therapies reinforce each other and, conversely, that there are also treatments which are better not to combine. When overseeing the entire spectrum of therapeutic measures, the right measure must be observed. A shortage of therapy does little justice to the self-healing potential of the organism; and vice versa, excess harms.

With the right effort, a start is already made with what comes to full fruition with the right remembrance: the examination. Here is sowed what can be harvested in the following exercise

In the event of a jointly established treatment by a therapeutical team (in a hospital or a health centre), one often arrives at an overarching leitmotif. This has the overview character of the right effort. When looking for such a comprehensive point of view, the group finds a higher law on the basis of the experience of the individual members. It goes without saying that one wishes to try out the reality of this idea in the light of the therapeutic effect. The group has thus made a start with conducting research.

7. With the **right remembrance** the real evaluation takes place. This seventh step of the Eightfold Path is taken when practising the retrospective review. For many people this exercise forms the beginning of the schooling way. It places, as it were, the foundation which can be built on further. While doing the retrospective review, one slows down the course of events, brings them to a halt and goes back in time. This reverse movement in the recollection, which runs contrary to the natural course of time, intensifies the power of the conscious mind. On the one hand, by making yourself more conscious of past observations, the alertness that is needed to perceive—also towards the future—increases. On the other hand, a process of evaluation develops, regarding what has happened: the essential is being distinguished from the unessential. Painful events are not suppressed, but are dealt with. They are being integrated into the biography. In most cases you appear—by coming to terms with these events—to have learnt something. Special events may have completely absorbed you when they took place. When they light up in your memory once again, by means of the retrospective review, they can have the effect of making you more attentive to comparable moments. You harvest these, as it were, not just in the evening when doing the retrospective review, but experience them with presence of mind at the moment itself. Looking at the past prepares you for being present in the future. In this way, life itself becomes a learning process.

You can, however, arrange life at certain places and moments in a way that will advance this learning process. That is by carrying out research. On the basis of specific questions, you carry out specific actions which you then assess—to learn from them. This is a way of working whereby you direct yourself to the course of events to a large extent. A possibility which forms a polarity to this, but is also complementary, takes place when you look at spontaneous actions that are being carried out, because life presents you with certain, in most cases, existential encounter situations. The retrospective review offers then the 'unexpectedly successful actions'. (See Albert de Vries' *Ervaringsleren cultiveren. Onderzoek in eigen werk.* Uitgeverij Eburon. Translated: *Cultivating learning experiences. Research in own work.*). Bringing to the surface the retrospective review, these spontaneously successful actions are a source of joy. What is even more important, however, is to understand why the action was successful. Only then will you have learnt through this retrospective review, and if it was the 'right remembrance'. In this way, other people can also make use of the insight which you have gained through this action.

8. As an exercise, **the right contemplation** has to wait until after the preceding seven steps have been set and experienced. This eighth step encompasses the previous exercises (in the same manner as the sixth *Nebenübung* (parallel exercise) makes the other five into a coherent fabric). This last exercise has no relation to a special day of the week; it stands, as it were, above time and serves on the one hand one's personal inner reflection. You are looking at yourself. What is the meaning and the purpose of my life? What are my priorities? Am I carrying out my intentions? On the other hand, the right contemplation focuses on the world and the position of human beings in the world: the evolution of Earth and human beings; the laws of karma; the development of the soul in the biography; and so on. There is specific literature to help with the inner transition of these matters, ranging from the anthroposophical basic works, the New Testament, works from earlier cultural epochs such as the story of Percival, to modern literature—writers such as Antoine de Saint-Exupéry, Thornton Wilder, and others. In patient libraries contemporary literature, as well as informative books about certain specific diseases, can provide nutriment and encouragement for patients in making their biographical journey. It goes without saying that specific meditations to suit the physician/therapist play an important role in practising the right contemplation.

How Does the Eightfold Path Work?

The exercises of the Eightfold Path purify the astral body and make it more human. This allows for the 'right communication' which lives within the message of the Buddha: love and compassion.

The so-called 'pedagogical law', discussed by Rudolf Steiner in his Curative Pedagogy Course indicates that in each individual there is an impact of the higher essential parts of the being on the lower essential parts. The 'I' has an impact on the soul (astral body), the soul on the life organism (etheric body), and finally the etheric body on the physical body. However, the essential being of the pedagogue impacts on the essential part of the being of the child that is beneath it. The 'I' of the adult (the parent or the teacher) works in on the soul of the child. The etheric body of the educator works in on the physical body of the child.

In adult life this is much less the case, unless somebody opens himself or herself in full confidence and surrender to the care and counsel of somebody else. This is, for instance, the case in a therapeutical situation. This perspective casts a new light on the question: what significance does the Eightfold Path have in the therapeutic profession? The purified and harmonized astral body of the therapist will have a wholesome influence on the etheric body of the patient.

The Relation to the Days of the Week

To see the relation to the days of the week, and the planets connected therewith, is sometimes difficult but in most cases evident.

- The question arises, for instance, why the first exercise falls on Saturday. This is probably connected with the fact that the Eightfold Path originated in pre-Christian times, when it was not the Sunday but the Saturday which formed the beginning of the week. In many cultures to the east of Europe, this is still the case. Saturn stood in any case at the start of Creation, which was repeated in the first post-Atlantean cultural period, the Old Indian culture, when a new consciousness awakened. Our thinking consciousness starts with the right view.

- Sunday as the day that is linked with the right judgement and the right resolve is a meaningful experience. The thinking light which has been ignited on Saturday is directed on Sunday towards the future. It is the day when we preview the coming week, focus on this internally, and take 'sunny' decisions.

- For the first time on Monday, something presents itself to the outside; plans are being communicated.

- Tuesday is the day of Mars, the day on which things are done. Many people know the problem (almost literally) of things getting out of hand exactly on a Tuesday. You warn each other: 'Watch it! It is Tuesday today. Avoid the occurrence of quarrels. Hold the action back a little longer, if necessary.'

- Wednesday owes its name to Mercury (*Mercredi*). It is the day of the encounter. It calls for the art of finding the right standpoint, gearing up to what is coming towards you, and not to push your own intentions but to act as an intermediary for what can be born from the constellation of that moment. Mercury is a fast planet. We may have to change our standpoint very quickly for the situation to remain fruitful.

- The day of Jupiter, Thursday, is devoted to the longer term strivings. The orbiting time of Jupiter is twelve years, while in one year Mercury rotates round the sun three times! It is important to see the interaction in time and to look after the continuity in our action. The right effort calls for some perseverance.

- Friday is the day which almost forms the end of the week. In the Christian tradition, Good Friday stands for remembering the moment when, for mankind, a new future began. On Friday, past and present are interconnected. We look back on the experiences of the past in order to create on that basis a new future. The retrospective review, which is needed particularly for this Friday activity, can be the stepping stone towards the right contemplation. This exercise is, however, not linked with a certain day, but can be connected to the inner attitude of each day.

The Sixth Century BC: The 'Hinge' of Time

The Eightfold Path was inaugurated by the Buddha in the sixth century before the start of the Christian calendar. This path was meant to lead to the development of compassion and love. These powers were not only practised in Asia, but also elsewhere in the world the impulse awoke for these capacities to germinate within the soul. One of the places where this schooling motive also lived was Ephesus. In this mystery centre, situated on the Aegean Sea, at the border of Asia and Europe, the transition from the old to the new consciousness was being guided. In the preceding time, man was still completely under the direction of the gods. Now he gradually grew into the situation where he began to assume responsibility for his own deeds. It was no longer the Furies, goddesses of wrath, who immediately appeared whenever man did something wrong. The spiritual world which, until that time, had always been perceptible became invisible and inaudible. However, in man himself a new capacity germinated. He now perceived something inside: he heard the voice of his conscience sound in his inner self. It is remarkable how at this moment in the evolution of man other skills are also born which were not there previously. The philosopher Karl Jaspers calls this phase in history the *Achsenzeit* ('time axis'). These growing inner capacities formed the hinge, the 'axis', which enabled a change of direction, a turn around. In relation to the world, man progressed into a new direction.

In Greek philosophy the power of wonder forms the beginning of a new way of thinking.

In the Greek dramas (Sophocles, Aeschylus, Euripides) the Erinyes (the Furies), goddesses of wrath, appeared. They now made room for the inner power of the conscience, for which even a new word made its entrance into the language: 'syneidesis'. Conscience arises as a new motive for action and mobilizes the will. Experiencing morality awakens the sense of responsibility for one's own deeds. Man becomes the custodian of the will.

As much as wonder makes the 'I' active in our thinking, conscience has this effect on our willing. Likewise, compassion and, out of this, love arise through the power of the 'I' in our feeling towards the world.

Wonder, compassion and conscience create together a constellation that did not previously exist. You could say that together they form the channel through which a new development can begin to stream. With all three powers, man actively creates a relationship with the world around him. In man's relation to his fellow beings and to the earth, from this moment onwards originates the possibility of individual initiative.